# DEDICATION

To my husband, Jeff, for always supporting me
with my choices so I can do the work
God intended me to do!

My Magical Choices
The Magic of Me Series

Copyright @ 2020 Becky Cummings

www.authorbcummings.com

ISBN: 978-1-7325963-6-8 (hardcover)
ISBN: 978-1-7325963-7-5 (ebook)

Library of Congress Control Number: 2019907988

Illustrations by Zuzana Svobodová
Book design by Zuzana Svobodová, Maškrtáreň
Editing by Tamara Rittershaus

Printed in the USA
Signature Book Printing

First printing edition 2019.

Free Kids Press

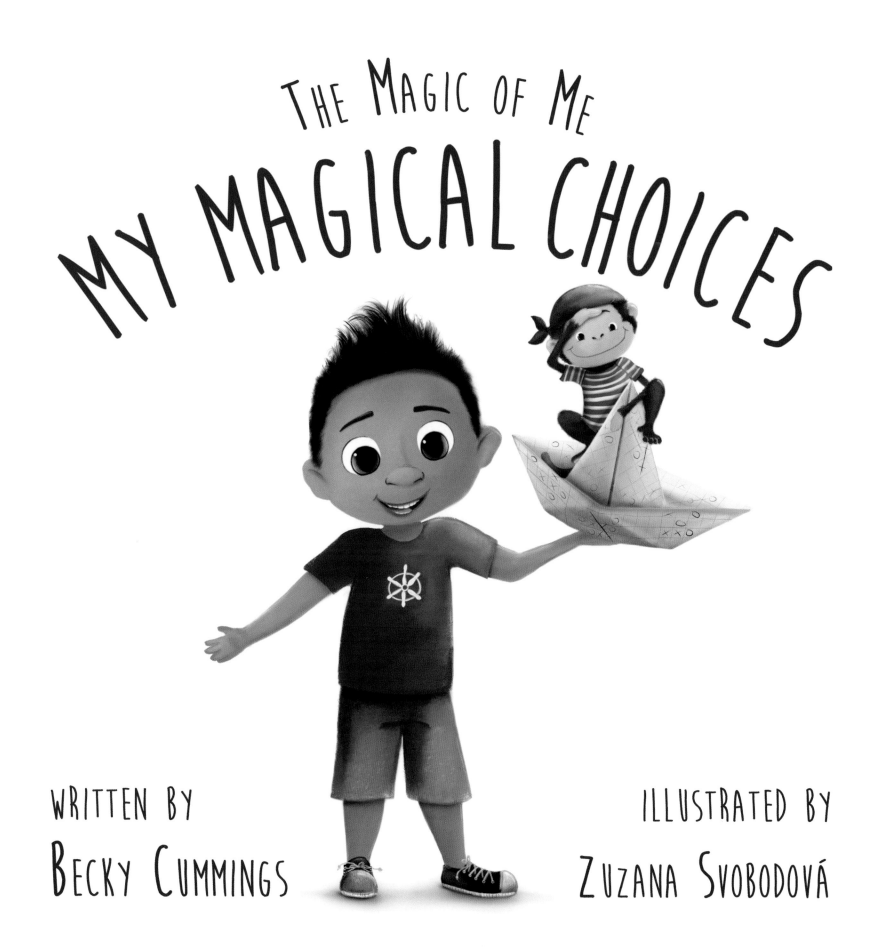

# The Magic of Me
# My Magical Choices

WRITTEN BY
BECKY CUMMINGS

ILLUSTRATED BY
ZUZANA SVOBODOVÁ

The choices you make have super powers!

They bring sunshine or rainy showers.

So here are some magical things to do,

that bring the sun to shine right through!

Listen closely to this life advice.

Say, 'I choose' and end with something nice!

Take some action, choose what you do.

Repeat this often, because

# MAGIC LIVES IN YOU!

# I choose to be responsible!

Bathing, brushing, getting dressed,
now you look and feel your best!
You clean up all the mess you make,
helping out gives mom or dad a break.

# I choose to be helpful!

Put toys away and feed the cat,

you might just like a job like that.

Just raise your hand or jump right in,

when helping others, we all win!

# I choose to be patient!

Take your time and wait your turn.

Those are tricky things to learn.

When life is slow, you've got to wait.

Stay calm and know

## IT TURNS OUT GREAT!

# I choose to be confident!

You know you can, you believe in you,
all by yourself, you try something new.
You don't give up when things get rough.
You know you're made to **BE SUPER TOUGH!**

# I choose to be generous!

Giving gifts for
no reason at all,
a cupcake, a flower,
maybe a ball.
Donating books,
clothes, or a toy,
fills your heart
with bursts of joy.

# I choose to be calm!

When you're upset, count to ten,
or take a break, then try again.
If still you feel you're sad and blue,
take a calming breath or two.

# I choose to be brave!

You speak what's important, kind, and true.

Your heart leads the way and knows what to do.

You try new things with a good attitude.

You do it politely, without being rude!

# I choose to be forgiving!

If something makes you feel so sad,

use words to explain the hurt you had.

Then it's okay to let these feelings go.

Heal your heart and let your smile show!

# I choose to be a good sport!

Play a game and try to have fun.

Say, "good job" when it's all done!

At times you win, at times you lose,

your attitude is what

YOU CHOOSE!

# I choose to be gentle!

Use your hands with grace and care.

Be kind to pets when stroking their hair.

With little friends you're careful too,

nobody wants to get a

BOO-BOO!

# I choose to be friendly !

You say hello to new people you meet.

You give high fives or handshakes to greet.

You use kind words with sisters and brothers.

You show respect to fathers and mothers.

# I choose to be honest!

Mistakes are part of everyday.

They help you learn a better way.

Just say you're sorry. Make it right.

The truth will make your

HEART FEEL LIGHT.

# I choose to be fun!

You play, you dance, you joke, you sing.

You enjoy what each moment may bring.

You do not need to follow the crowd,

be silly, be you and

## LAUGH OUT LOUD!

You are the captain of your own ship.

You steer the wheel on this magic trip.

So wisely choose the things you do!

And always remember

MAGIC STARTS IN YOU!

SPECIAL AS CAN BE

# THIS IS THE

# MAGIC OF ME!

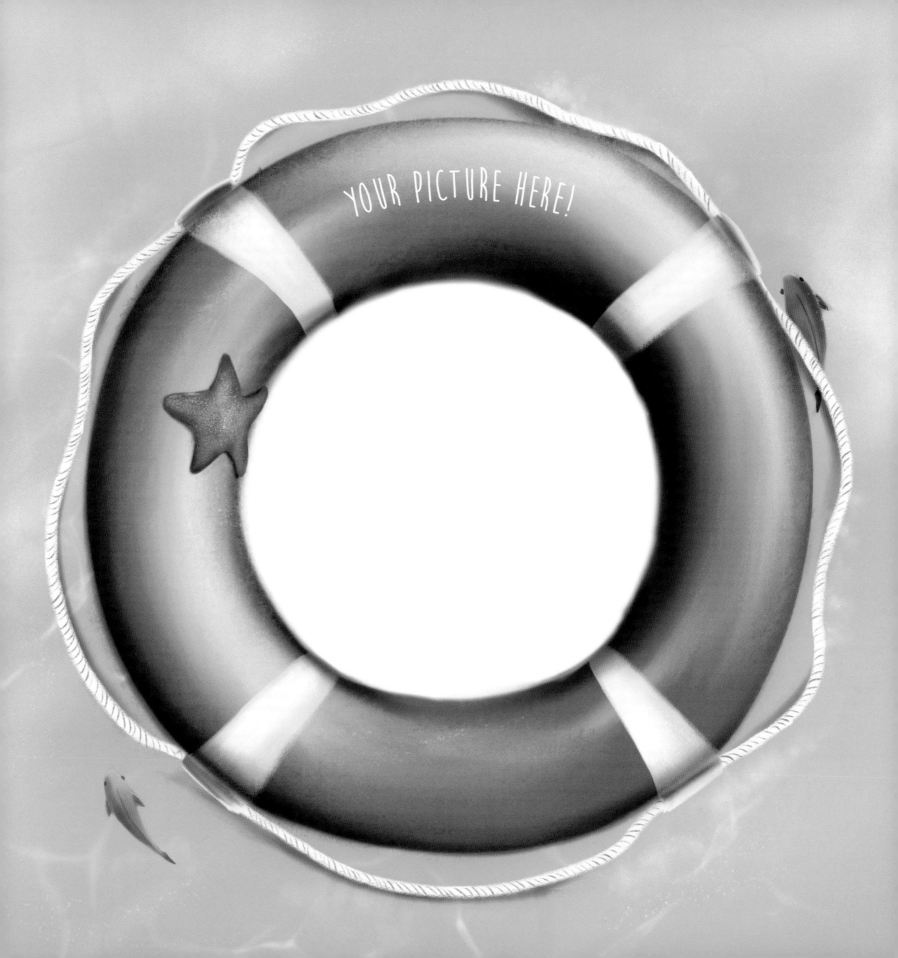

# TIPS FOR READING WITH CHILDREN

- Have children repeat the positive choice after you.

- Create an action to go with each positive choice. For example, after reading, "I choose to be friendly," make up a special handshake you can do together.

- Ask children to give other examples that show the positive choice in action. For example, after reading the page about responsibility, ask children to share other ways they can show they are responsible.

# ENJOY MORE BOOKS IN THIS SERIES BY BECKY CUMMINGS!

www.authorbcummings.com